MW01248586

UN-UNITED

UN-UNITED

Written by
Timothy Harvey

Hardback ISBN: 979-8-8692-9390-9
Paperback ISBN: 979-8-8692-9071-7
E-Book: 979-8-8692-9384-8

Published in United States of America

10 9 8 7 6 5 4 3 2 1

VMH Publishing
New York, NY - Atlanta, GA

Table of Contents

Introduction:

In his poignant and thought-provoking book, "Un-United," Timothy Harvey invites readers on a compelling exploration of America's social fabric. With a thoughtful blend of personal anecdotes, historical insights, and societal reflections, "Un-United" navigates through the complexities of race, politics, and social disparities. It challenges readers to confront uncomfortable truths and envision a future where unity is not just a distant dream but a tangible reality.

From historical injustices to present-day challenges, this book seeks to illuminate the path towards healing and unity. Through compelling narratives and thought-provoking analysis, this book sparks conversations about accountability, justice, and the collective responsibility to create a more inclusive society. "Un-United" is a call to action, urging individuals to embrace change, confront bias, and work towards a shared vision of a brighter, more united America.

CHAPTER 1

ACHIEVING THE DREAM BUILT FROM THE ASHES OF A NIGHTMARE

The American Dream symbolizes the hope and desire of every human being across the globe. For many, it's hard to fathom that a place founded on such fundamental principles like equality, democracy, liberty, individual prosperity, and success could truly exist. The United States of America stands as a shining beacon atop a hill, embodying the most cherished values of life, liberty, and the pursuit of happiness.

At one point, this was also my vision, and I held onto it with every fiber of my being. However, life has a way of unraveling secrets and reshaping one's perspectives and beliefs. The reality is that for African American individuals, the very American Dream we celebrate today was made possible through the nightmare of slavery. Well before the nation was established and secured its independence from the British, African Americans were traded and sold worldwide. Many pivotal moments in history have been reinterpreted to align with the narrative of the American Dream.

One such story that comes to mind involves Francis Scott Key and the credit attributed to him for writing the Star-Spangled Banner. The anthem, with its stirring melody and patriotic fervor, is often seen as a tribute to American resilience and strength. However, a significant flaw lies within this beloved national song—it serves as a reminder of one of the darkest chapters in our history.

Francis Scott Key, the author of the Star-Spangled Banner, was not only an anti-abolitionist but also a slave owner. The lyrics of the controversial third verse of this anthem depict the gruesome fate awaiting slaves who dared to seek freedom during wartime or refused to fight for their American masters against the British. For years, I remained unaware of the hypocrisy underlying this song. Once I uncovered the true meaning behind the lyrics, my perception of it and what it represents shifted entirely.

As a retired combat veteran with nearly 25 years of service, this realization hit me deeply. Like many fellow service members, veterans, and First Responders, this anthem had always resonated with me in a profound way that's hard to convey to those who haven't experienced it firsthand.

Today, I find myself conflicted about how I should feel about being patriotic or feeling allegiance to the flag. I love and will always love my country. My loyalty to this nation is unwavering. However, I believe I am equally bound to speak about the racial divide that has plagued this nation from its inception, and even more so today for some. Just as I served to promote, protect, and defend democracy domestically and abroad, it is disheartening to realize that there was never any plan for Black people to live freely as citizens with the same rights and liberties as those of our oppressors.

The idea of any Black American speaking about the truth and disparities of our nation has historically been met with character assassinations and labels of radicalism. Dr. Martin Luther King Jr.'s dream envisioned a nation that could and should reflect true American ideals. The Civil Rights Movement never aimed to secede from the Union or storm the capital to overthrow the government. Instead, it vigorously fought against discrimination and, more importantly, introduced legislative solutions that would benefit all Americans seeking fair and equal treatment regardless of color or gender. On a lighter note, if you'd like to vote for me now, I think I might have just subtly announced my candidacy for office.

However, reflecting on historical events, it's troubling that we often fail to consider the impact of symbols like national anthems. Have we become desensitized to its implications? Do our lawmakers even care about it? Has anyone recognized that this song may be offensive to Black people? Notably, the 1931 resolution passed by the U.S. Congress to designate this song as the National Anthem of the United States of America had no representation from African Americans or any people of color. I can't help but wonder what my fate would have been in 1931 if I, as a voting member of Congress, had opposed the lyrics of the third verse. Would there have been a national holiday celebrated in my honor back then? I highly doubt it.

Over the years, I've strived to put everything into perspective, focusing on deliberation in processing historical events and how they continue to impact America today. I begin by acknowledging that America was conceived out of wedlock. The American Dream was meant to unite the citizens of this nation in their pursuit of life, liberty, and happiness, with an inclusive governing body made for the people and by the people, ensuring equal opportunities for all who reside in this nation. If you're ready to delve into my musings, come in, pour yourself a coffee, and get comfortable.

The generational scars of slavery will probably never heal, in my opinion. Rape, torture, physical abuse, mental abuse, and human trafficking are just a few examples of what took place daily for centuries. If you happen to be white and are reading this, I will let you in on a little secret. The conversation about slavery is just as uncomfortable for most of us as it is for you. You do not bear the responsibility alone for combating racism; it is an American responsibility. This must be understood first and foremost. These are merely my thoughts based on historical facts.

Let's imagine if things began differently for a moment. Imagine the birth of America and a democracy formed that was inclusive to African Americans and Native Americans. The cultural ignorance of not recognizing that despite differences in languages, culture, and even religious beliefs were all ingredients in this Gumbo called democracy. Slavery did not afford us the opportunity to become that indivisible nation. Slave traders and slave owners created generational wealth from the labor of other human beings who also had mothers, fathers, sons, and daughters. Slaves were regarded as less than human.

Back to my original "What if" scenario. Can you imagine the contributions of African and Native American farmers, doctors, engineers, carpenters, and scientists, just to name a few, living free as citizens in the newly formed United States of America? One could only imagine the impact of the contributions it may have had on society, right?

America did indeed get a chance to experience this. But before I get to that, I want to talk more about how this all started. Going back to that iconic story of the image of the flag flying in the distance over the battleground that inspired the composition of the lyrics to the Star-Spangled Banner highlights one of the great moments in American History. The war would end with the signing of the Treaty of Ghent in December 1814, but officially ended with the ratification of the treaty by the United States Congress on February 17, 1815.

The untold or unpublished part of this story is the role slavery played in all of this. Remember the lyrics of the third verse of the Star-Spangled Banner and how it spoke to the demise of those slaves that would try to flee or oppose the commands of their masters to fight? I will shed light on this quickly. At the forefront of it all was slavery. A vast majority of the foot soldiers engaging in daily deadly confrontations with the enemy were supported logistically by slaves. They were loyal servants to their masters and were giving their lives to defend a nation that bought and sold them as expendable property.

Seeing a pattern here? There is much more. It would be less than one hundred years later that the legacy of slavery would become prominent. The contributions of Black people began to hold more significance. Black inventors, such as Benjamin Montgomery, born into slavery in 1819, invented a steamboat propeller designed for shallow waters. Another notable figure is Thomas Jennings, the first Black Patent Holder, who invented dry cleaning in 1821. While there are many more examples I could speak of, the point is clear. For some Americans, the realization of democracy could not be possible without the contributions of all citizens.

These Americans, also known as abolitionists, faced fierce opposition. Those opposed to abolishing slavery viewed the emerging incredible contributions of former slaves as threats to white supremacy, an economy primarily based on agriculture (specifically cotton), and a plantation system fueled by slave labor. It became a crossroads in America.

The issue of slavery tore the nation apart. Greed, power, and hate unleashed destructive forces that swept uncontrollably through the country. Southern states like South Carolina, Mississippi, Florida, Alabama, Georgia, Louisiana, Texas, Virginia, Arkansas, Tennessee, and North Carolina united efforts to form the Confederate States of America. Their goal was the preservation of slavery at any cost, beginning with seceding from the Union on February 8,

1861. The Civil War erupted shortly after on April 12, 1861, with the Confederate attack on Union Soldiers at Fort Sumter, South Carolina.

Once again, I want to delve into the details. It's important to note that slavery had not yet been abolished in the country. Black people were exploited to further the goals of both sides during this war. Free Black men and women were compelled to take up arms and fight for the Union, while slaves, mainly in the South, were coerced by their masters (akin to previous wars) to fight to maintain their enslavement.

It's indeed a complex and often overlooked part of history. Many have been led to believe that the North was solely focused on abolishing slavery. Abraham Lincoln is often credited with the abolition of slavery, but a quote from his inaugural address sheds light on a different perspective. He stated, "No amendment shall be made to the Constitution, which will authorize or give the Congress the power to abolish or interfere within any State, with the domestic institutions thereof, including that of the persons held to labor or service by the laws of said State." This part of history is not widely referenced. Those words were his formal endorsement of the resolution passed by the 36th Congress on March 2nd, 1861, which aimed to bring back the seceding states to the Union and persuade the border slave states to remain (this was known as the Corwin Amendment).

Here is where things become complicated for Lincoln. The resolution needed to be ratified by a required number of states, and if done before 1865, it would have made institutionalized slavery immune to constitutional amendment procedures and any congressional oversight or intervention. It's a lot to process. Perhaps a coffee break or something stronger is in order by now.

We owe a great deal of gratitude to abolitionists like Frederick Douglass who emerged from the shadows of slavery with minimal education and rose to become a prominent activist, author, and public speaker. He dedicated his life before and after the Civil War to the abolition of slavery and the fight for equal rights for Black people. Douglass stands out as one of the most intriguing figures I will touch on. His transformation from a slave with limited education to an accomplished author and renowned public speaker in a divided nation speaks volumes about the resilience of Black people.

When I consider this man who was once enslaved, described as having limited education, and yet managed to carve out a path to success as an influential figure in a fractured society, it highlights the incredible resilience and determination of Black individuals. Despite being stripped of their culture, language, heritage, and dignity upon arrival as slaves, figures like Douglass not only survived but thrived, paving the way for change. One can only imagine the immense obstacles he had to overcome on his journey as a former slave.

Abolitionists faced fierce opposition, yet it is important to note that the spirit of America was beginning to reveal itself. It would be remiss of me not to acknowledge the efforts of other abolitionists such as John Quincy Adams, the sixth President of the United States (1825-1829). During his presidency, the House of Representatives overturned the practice known as the Gag Rule, which forbade addressing petitions to abolish slavery. This reversal allowed abolitionists in government and private citizens to openly oppose slavery without fear of legal or political repercussions.

History can lead us down various paths, and I understand that this particular journey has been full of twists and turns so far. Now that you're on your second drink, let's delve into this further, shall we? Is it possible that if that resolution had passed, slavery would still exist? Here's my perspective: it might have continued, albeit under a different guise.

In the Reconstruction Era, African American individuals began to gain rights due to the passage of three amendments to the United States Constitution aimed at newly freed slaves. These were known as the Reconstruction Amendments or the Civil War Amendments, passed between 1865 and 1870. The 13th Amendment, proposed in 1864 and ratified in 1865, abolished slavery and involuntary servitude, with exceptions for those duly convicted of a crime. The 14th Amendment, proposed in 1866 and ratified in 1868, addressed citizenship rights and equal protection under the law for all individuals. Finally, the 15th Amendment, proposed in 1869 and ratified in 1870, prohibited discrimination in voting based on race, color, or previous servitude. Despite these advancements, tactics like poll taxes, literacy tests, and intimidation were used to control people of color.

The conditions for African American individuals during that time were eerily similar to issues we face today, particularly surrounding immigration. As slaves sought freedom from the perils of slavery by migrating north, the strain on the Union was significant. Efforts were made to reorganize captured territories with legislation aimed at protecting the rights of people of color. It's important to remember that slavery had not yet been fully abolished, and Congress was hesitant to intervene in matters related to its removal or interference with the institution itself.

However, the realization that this system was unsustainable became apparent. The nation could not function as two separate entities, and the end of institutionalized slavery became inevitable. Two critical pieces of legislation in 1861 and 1862, known as the Confiscation Acts, played a significant role in weakening the institution of slavery. The first, passed on August 6th, 1861, allowed Union forces to confiscate Confederate property, including slaves. The second act, passed on July 17th, 1862, stated that any Confederate military or civilian official who did not surrender within 60 days would have their slaves freed. This provision only applied to Confederate states already occupied by the Union Army.

Okay, that turned into a full-fledged research paper! It's fascinating how history unfolds. Alexa, please return to the previous route!

The Emancipation Proclamation, officially known as Proclamation 95, stands as a pivotal legislation that solidified President Abraham Lincoln's legacy. I believe that responsibility and credibility stem from accountability. Initially, Lincoln supported a resolution that refrained from intervening in state laws supporting slavery. This was a strategic move to dissuade border states from joining the Confederacy and to bring back seceding states into the Union. He deserves credit for recognizing the country's trajectory. The Emancipation Proclamation fundamentally altered the legal status of over three million enslaved African Americans, freeing them primarily in the southeastern United States. It's crucial to note that while impactful, the Emancipation Proclamation was not the sole legislation responsible for ending slavery, akin to the climax of a season finale—provocative and uncertain.

Subsequently, what challenges would the nation encounter due to these changes? What does emancipation truly signify? The term "emancipated" describes one who is free from legal, social, or political constraints. Despite its clear definition, the word has subtly shifted in meaning over time, becoming a convenient or opportunistic term. Delving into cultural references, allow me to say, "Let me lay down the boogie" from the 70s (revealing a bit of my age there).

The concept of emancipation resonates with the essence of democracy, reflecting visions, ideologies, sustainability, and equality. However, it presents a paradox with the American spirit. Some may wonder about the distinction between spirit and soul. To me, the spirit of democracy embodies vision and values, while the soul reflects our collective identity. It exists both as a culmination and a singular entity. The soul of America remains accountable, perpetually striving to align with the spirit of democracy. From my perspective, African Americans have yet to fully realize emancipation based on its definition. The evolution of America's soul is apparent, but the enduring legacy of slavery and its aftermath remains a prominent aspect of its character.

The nation struggled to accept African Americans as equals despite the reunification of seceding states with the Union. After centuries of operating within a certain framework, global shifting occurred as former slaves, once carpenters, blacksmiths, or farmers, now posed as competition. The rise of inventive black individuals posed a threat to the established white hierarchy.

The Reconstruction era marked what I consider the second chapter of subjugation for African Americans. They were not embraced as full citizens of the United States. Shockingly, the average life expectancy for African Americans was around 33 years, with 9 out of 10 residing in the South, and approximately 44.5 percent being illiterate. Despite the lack of educational funding and opportunities for young black children to attend public schools on par with their white counterparts, the resilience of African

Americans in overcoming these challenges is nothing short of remarkable.

Consider this perspective: the illiteracy label placed on African Americans disregarded the fact that they had to adapt to a new language and culture in a foreign land where they were enslaved for generations. Branding them as illiterate was a deliberate tactic to enforce white superiority and dehumanize an entire race. It's crucial to push back against this narrative. Prior to colonization, African kingdoms thrived with sophisticated cities, distinct languages, cultures, monarchies, and intricate political systems governing vast populations. The vast social structures, innovative contributions, and ingenuity of African Americans were systematically overlooked from the outset.

Over time, talented African Americans seized opportunities to pursue their passions and rise above adversity. The adage "when you know, you grow" rings true, highlighting the importance of education as a pathway to success.

As we continue our journey through history, I suggest it might be a good time for you to grab a fresh cup of coffee or any other drink you prefer. All settled in? Great!

Let's delve into the Greenville District of Tulsa, OK, also known as the Greenwood District or Black Hollywood. At the turn of the 20th century, Greenwood District stood out as one of the most significant hubs of African American businesses in the United States. Perhaps you've come across this story before, but I'll give you a brief summary as some details are crucial.

It all began during Memorial Day weekend when a 19-year-old black shoe shiner named Dick Rowland was accused of assaulting a 17-year-old white girl named Sarah Page, who worked as an elevator operator in a nearby building. Subsequently, he was taken into custody, and a white mob gathered outside the jail with intentions to lynch him in what they perceived as justice for the alleged assault. This narrative bears a striking resemblance to past events, a sadly familiar and somber occurrence. But I digress.

A group of African American residents from the Greenwood District arrived at the jail to shield the young man, believing him to be falsely accused. Amidst this tension, a white citizen demanded that a Greenwood resident relinquish his firearm. The refusal led to a scuffle in which the gun accidentally discharged, sparking a riot. Realizing they were outnumbered, the African American residents withdrew to the Greenwood District. Later that weekend, the white mob was deputized by the local sheriff's department and descended upon the Greenwood District, ravaging black residential homes and businesses, ultimately obliterating over thirty-five square blocks of what was once one of the most affluent black communities in the U.S.

Opinions vary on these events, and though I steer clear of conspiracy theories, I'll stick to presenting some straightforward facts. White residents felt threatened by the prosperity, growth, and size of what was referred to as Black Wall Street in the Greenwood District, which began encroaching into white neighborhoods. What remains profoundly tragic about this incident is the overshadowed grim reality that thirty-nine individuals lost their lives, 39 fellow Americans. Thirteen of the deceased were white, and twenty-six were African Americans. More than eight hundred people were admitted to hospitals, six thousand were displaced for days (with many left homeless), and the district was left in ruins following one of the most brutal racial assaults in American history.

Recalling our previous discussion on the outset of Reconstruction, we touched upon the emergence of state and local laws in the Southern United States towards the turn of the century that sought to enforce segregation. Despite the South's defeat in the Civil War, there was a persistent defiance in their attempts to assert a sense of superiority over their now fellow U.S. citizens. These laws came to be known as the Jim Crow Laws. Brace yourself for some unsettling and distasteful truths.

The character of Jim Crow was first brought to life by an itinerant white actor named Thomas Dartmouth in 1830. Essentially, this individual would don blackface and imitate aspects of African American culture and race in what was deemed as entertainment. Portraying a dim-witted buffoon, he engaged in activities aimed at generating laughter. I'd rather not give any more attention or time to this dark chapter. Let's press forward.

To me, the essence behind Jim Crow can be likened to a distorted notion of equality. The fundamental premise behind the implementation of these laws was "separate but equal." However, the reality painted a different picture. Public facilities and transportation meant for African Americans were consistently subpar and inadequately funded compared to those reserved for white Americans. In some cases, there were no facilities allocated for the black community at all. The Jim Crow Laws entrenched economic, educational, political, and social disparities, rendering African Americans essentially as second-class citizens, at least until the moment they were deemed necessary.

Amidst the backdrop of World War I, significant changes were witnessed in the draft process. Prior exclusions and discriminatory practices against black individuals seeking to enlist in the military suddenly saw a shift. Representation of African Americans on draft boards was nonexistent, with these boards being exclusively composed of white men. Interestingly, African American land and business owners with families were often prioritized in the draft ahead of white single males. Additionally, reports surfaced of Southern postal workers purposely withholding registration cards of eligible black men, leading to their arrest on charges of draft evasion. Despite these challenges, over 350,000 African Americans valiantly served in World War I, highlighting their unwavering commitment and sacrifice during a tumultuous period in history.

During World War II, over a million African American men and women patriotically served in the United States Armed Forces. Despite their dedication and sacrifices, the systemic inequities persisted, perpetuating a narrative of inequality. These courageous African American individuals showcased unwavering loyalty and honor in defense of what the world perceived as a beacon of hope. Among them, the Tuskegee Airmen, a group of African American pilots, garnered acclaim for their exceptional combat prowess in safeguarding American bombers from enemy threats during the war. Yet, even amidst their remarkable military achievements, the shadow of Jim Crow continued to loom over the South, reflecting a harsh reality.

However, a breakthrough emerged. In 1948, President Harry S. Truman took a historic step by signing Executive Order 9981, thus dismantling segregation within the military. This significant milestone in history marked a pivotal shift towards inclusivity and equality within the armed forces, a turning point worthy of remembrance.

Beyond the military sphere, the era continued to bear witness to a consistent pattern in our history - the relentless battle against segregation and racial injustice unfolded across the nation. Confronting the deeply rooted laws of Jim Crow and systemic discrimination demanded a different approach, one rooted in strategic and psychological warfare to minimize harm and preserve resources, as articulated in Sunzi's "The Art of War."

Introducing the champion gearing up to dismantle racial segregation, discrimination, and disenfranchisement through nonviolent resistance and civil disobedience: The Civil Rights Movement! *Applause fills the air.*

The Civil Rights Movement, a pivotal social campaign, primarily thrived between 1954 and

1968. Notably, the movement had previous incarnations in two distinct eras - from 1865 to 1896 and from 1896 to 1954. The earlier phase aimed at eradicating racial discrimination against African Americans, enhancing their access to education and employment opportunities, and bolstering their political representation immediately following the abolition of slavery in the United States. The subsequent era from 1896 to 1954 centered on nonviolent activism to secure civil rights and legal equality for all Americans, transcending racial barriers in pursuit of justice and harmony.

I have had the pleasure, as I am sure you have also, of speaking to family members who lived through this historical time in America. The takeaway for me was the consistency of each story I heard regarding how race was at the center of everything. By some accounts, it was just as bad if not worse than the Civil War. African Americans were being lynched and brutalized at the hands of elected law enforcement officials. The Southern States were playing by their own rules and blatantly disregarding federal laws governing segregation and discrimination.

My mother described the Civil Rights Era as the war between the races. The banter throughout the South, rallying around the Confederate Flag, gave those who wished to support and defend white supremacy a voice that could be heard across the country. At the center of it all, or what some would describe as the proverbial shot around the country, was when a 14-year-old African American boy was abducted, tortured, and lynched in Mississippi in 1955 after being accused of offending a white woman and her family's grocery store. His name was Emmett Till.

The details of this young man's murder are gruesome, but I want to direct your attention to the intent behind it all. If you have not read the story, I would encourage you to do so. My summary of events is as follows: Emmett Till was visiting from Chicago to Mississippi. He spoke to a young lady, and the Good Old Boys decided that he had no right to do so. In the South, it was an unwritten rule that white women were forbidden fruit for African Americans. Again, before we continue, let us remember – Emmett Till was 14 years old! The lady's name was Carolyn Bryant. She was 21 years old and the proprietor of the grocery store.

Returning to the original point of intent, in 2017, an author and historian named Timothy Tyson released some details of a 2008 interview with Carolyn Bryant where he alleged that she recanted her story, stating that parts of her testimony during trial were fabricated. This is important to know because it sheds light on how lawless and un-united the country was at that moment in time. After several days, Carolyn Bryant's husband and stepbrother went to Emmett Till's great uncle's house and abducted him. This was a premeditated act of kidnapping, assault, torture, and murder.

Can you believe it? For the sake of argument, let's consider a disagreement of some sort. In the deep South at that time, I'm sure Emmett was given briefings on how to navigate his visit from Chicago. The racial tension was as thick as a kindergarten number two pencil. Excuse my Southern humor, but you get what I'm saying, right?

Those men were filled with rage and wanted to assert themselves as White Supremacists. Here's more on their intent: the two men were arrested, but the justice system favored them. In Mississippi, the only three outcomes possible for capital murder were life imprisonment, the death penalty, or acquittal. The defense attorney claimed that the events of the night Emmett Till was murdered were improbable. He argued to the jury that their forefathers would turn over in their graves if they convicted these men. Women and all Black people were prohibited from being jurors in this trial, so the all-white male jury acquitted both men after only a 67-minute deliberation. One juror even commented, "If we hadn't stopped to drink pop, it wouldn't have taken that long." Some jurors believed the men were guilty but didn't think life imprisonment or the death penalty were fitting punishments for killing a Black man. It seems the two men had supreme confidence that they would never be held accountable for their heinous acts.

Emmett Till's tragic death would not be in vain. It is heralded as one of the most iconic events of the Civil Rights Movement. His death fueled a campaign drawing attention to the long history of violent persecution of African Americans in the United States.

From the ashes of a jaded race of people arose some of the most courageous and influential leaders in American history. It is well-documented that Dr. Martin Luther King Jr., along with Malcolm X, the Black Panthers, and several other great leaders, dedicated their lives to ending segregation and abolishing Jim Crow laws. The opposition each of these brave leaders had to face was either initiated, sanctioned, or supported by the very establishment responsible for change.

Thankfully, cynicism did not derail their efforts in a time when it seemed as if at every turn, they were fighting an uphill battle. Excuse my blunt remarks, but the irony in that statement couldn't be clearer. J. Edgar Hoover, who served nearly 50 years as the director of the Federal Bureau of

Investigation, was once asked, "what was the single greatest threat to the United States of America?" Without hesitation, he answered, "Negro Unity." I'll take a leap here and suggest that Hoover recognized that not only was the prevailing situation in America wrong, but also that he came to realize that if Americans united, equality was possible. The writing was on the wall—the Civil Rights Movement was gaining the support of Americans of all races. The defense strategy was simple: discredit, disregard, disrespect, degrade, and dismantle all advancements toward equality and unity among races.

Tactics such as wiretapping and surveillance of key figures including the Southern Christian Leadership Conference, led by then President Rev Dr. Martin Luther King Jr., Dr. T.R.M Howard, a wealthy entrepreneur, surgeon, and civil rights activist who publicly criticized the FBI's inaction in solving the murders of George W. Lee, Emmett Till, and others in the South, as well as the Black Panthers and their leader Huey P. Newton, were employed. Supporters of White Nationalism found strength through the ideologies of Hoover and others who opposed the Civil Rights Movement. As peaceful protests against injustice and segregation became more common in the Jim Crow South, lawmakers began flexing their authority.

The Birmingham Campaign of 1963, involving coordinated marches and sit-ins against racism and segregation in Birmingham, was met with swift and aggressive legal retaliation. Circuit Judge W. A. Jenkins Jr. issued an injunction prohibiting assembling, boycotting, trespassing, and picketing in public places. Undeterred, Dr. King, alongside activists Ralph Abernathy and Fred Shuttlesworth, backed by the First Amendment of the United States Constitution, willfully disobeyed this unjust order.

The leaders and several others were arrested and taken to a harshly guarded Birmingham jail. An ally and supporter of the campaign managed to smuggle a newspaper inside to Dr. King. It contained a statement called "A Call to Unity" written by eight Alabama clergymen who opposed Dr. King and his methods. This was a show of force, a display of power to warn others against challenging them. However, they did not anticipate the bold response from Dr. King. The courage and determination that defined him were evident as he penned what would later be known as the famous Birmingham Letter. With intellectual prowess, he scrutinized and countered the deliberate intentions and gross negligence of those seeking to persecute peaceful citizens who sought change in a biased, segregated Jim Crow South upheld by a corrupt system. He emphasized the moral duty of all individuals to oppose unjust laws rather than passively waiting for congressional or judicial intervention through direct action. In one of my favorite statements from his response, he delivered a knockout blow, "Injustice anywhere is a threat to justice everywhere." MIC DROP!

This is the perfect time to point out that the Civil Rights Movement, although depicted as a battle for equality for African Americans, was a social movement for equality for all citizens of the United States.

Not everyone in the African American community agreed with the peaceful, nonviolent strategy for achieving justice and equality. The consequences of slavery and the generational trauma it left behind continue with the story of the Black Panther Party (originally called the Black Panther Party for Self-Defense). The party's central practice was its open-carry patrols in their respective neighborhoods, aimed at challenging and sometimes avenging excessive force and misconduct against African Americans by the Oakland Police Department in California. Founded by two college students, Bobby Seale and Huey P. Newton, in 1966, the party was labeled as a Marxist-Leninist Black power political organization.

Any means of resistance against political and social injustice was met with fierce opposition, as my grandmother often emphasized to us. Her signature saying was, "If you're gonna tell it, tell it all."

It's crucial to note some overlooked facts about this organization. The party operated for sixteen years (1966-1982) with chapters across major U.S. cities like San Francisco, New York City, Chicago, Los Angeles, Seattle, and Philadelphia. From a leadership standpoint alone, this is quite impressive. The party extended its influence into prisons nationwide and even had international chapters in the United Kingdom and Algeria. The underlying ideology aimed to provoke social change, evidenced by the creation of social programs including Free Breakfast for Children Programs, educational initiatives, and community health clinics where young African American men and women were taught skills to open businesses and develop community investment strategies.

However, this storyline isn't new to America, resonating with incidents like "Black Wall Street." J. Edgar Hoover, the Director of the FBI, famously cited the party as "the greatest threat to the internal security of the country." Hoover was vehement in his efforts to impede, if not dismantle, the momentum of this movement for equality. Through the Counterintelligence Program (COINTELPRO), the party was sabotaged with illegal and covert projects involving surveillance, infiltration, perjury, and police harassment to criminalize its activities.

The narrative takes a dark turn when, in 1969, the FBI played a role in the assassinations of Fred Hampton and Mark Clark during a raid by the Chicago Police Department. Behind the scenes, directives governing COINTELPRO—such as disruption, misdirection, illegal wiretapping, and neutralization of activities—were personally authorized by the United States Attorney General. These actions were not exclusive to the Black Panther Party but also targeted organizations like the Southern Leadership Conference, the Nation of Islam, the American Indian Movement, Puerto Rican Independence Groups, and various other minority groups fighting for social change and equality.

Before revealing the name of the Attorney General responsible for these directives and the wiretapping of Dr. Martin Luther King Jr.'s phones, it's worth noting that he approved limited wiretapping in hopes of finding incriminating evidence in any aspect of King's life. And the unexpected reveal is none other than Robert Francis Kennedy, also known as RFK.

History indeed shows that during his time in office, Robert F. Kennedy was known for advocating for the Civil Rights Movement. One might wonder, as he worked on human rights and social justice issues with Dr. Martin Luther King Jr. abroad in Eastern Europe, Latin America, and South Africa, did he ever disclose to Dr. King that his phone was being tapped? This revelation may seem contradictory to the image of him as an icon of modern American liberalism.

The title of the book, "Un-United," certainly hints at the disunity present in such situations. It's plausible to believe that Dr. King and others in his circle were aware of the surveillance they were under. In fact, after the 1963 assassination of John F. Kennedy, Dr. King expressed to his wife, Coretta Scott King, his premonition saying, "This is what is going to happen to me also. I keep telling you, this is a sick society." The pervasive surveillance and violent acts committed by the government, including the FBI, against African Americans and other minority groups made such suspicions quite reasonable.

Delving deeper into this unsettling reality, despite numerous documented cases of illegal activities like wiretapping, surveillance, bribery, extortion, blackmail, witness tampering, and even assassinations (such as during the Black

Panther raid by the Chicago Police) orchestrated under the joint direction of the United States Attorney General, Robert F. Kennedy, and the FBI Director, J. Edgar Hoover, over nearly five decades, no charges or indictments were brought against any of the perpetrators as far as my knowledge extends. This raises the incredulous question of how such impunity was possible.

American history carries a consistent thread of reprehensible discrimination against African American and minority citizens. Compounding this issue, many individuals responsible for such acts have been immortalized and honored in the most prestigious historical sites. The FBI Headquarters, for instance, bears the name of Hoover, perpetuating this discomforting reality.

This scenario might ring a bell when considering the nine significant Army military bases formerly named after Confederate military leaders during the World Wars, all hailing from Confederate States. Even the Arlington National Cemetery designates an area (Confederate Section 16) housing the graves of 482 Confederate Veterans and spouses. The presence of Confederate leaders and soldiers immortalized in statues within the Statuary Hall of the United States Capitol further highlights this deep-rooted issue. Across the United States, more than 1,500 public monuments and memorials pay tribute to the Confederacy, with a substantial portion located in Georgia, Virginia, and North Carolina.

The brazen displays of White Supremacy stemming from the darkest chapters of our history are not only permitted in America today but also celebrated nationwide for decades. It's incredulous to confront such symbols, particularly within revered institutions. Reflecting on a prior visit to the United States Capitol, I stumbled upon Statuary Hall and couldn't help but ponder how lawmakers could walk by these representations each day without evoking some form of unease. This deviates starkly from the ideals that America is purported to uphold.

One of the most confounding aspects for me is witnessing African Americans visiting and endorsing Stone Mountain Park. For those unfamiliar, it showcases the largest bias-relief sculpture globally, featuring carvings of three Confederate leaders of the Civil War on horseback—President Jefferson Davis, General Robert E. Lee, and Thomas J. "Stonewall" Jackson. The entire park serves as a commemoration to the Confederacy, with streets named after Confederate leaders and Confederate flags adorning every corner. Climbing to the apex, one encounters the site where the Ku Klux Klan convened, adding an unsettling layer to an already troubling narrative. To cap it off, visitors can explore the lavish Antebellum Plantation and Farmyard – a reconstruction of a pre-Civil War Georgia plantation. This setting appears tailor-made for individuals harboring racist ideologies and nostalgic sentiments for the 1860s.

Residing in the Atlanta-Metro area, I recoil at the mere thought of venturing there. The absence of any consideration for treason— defined as the crime of betraying one's country, particularly by plotting against the sovereign or subverting the government—in this context further exacerbates the disquiet, leaving me with a throbbing migraine.

Chapter 2

ONE COLOR, ONE GENDER

The Constitution of the United States of America was written to communicate the intentions of the framers of democracy. For the union to survive, it must adhere to those values and principles established as a solid foundation. I spoke earlier about the Spirit verses the Soul of America and what I felt were the differences.

The preamble is the embodied spirit of America. One voice with the collaboration of many for a common cause. It reads, "We the People of the United States, in Order to form a more perfect Union, establish Justice, ensure domestic Tranquility, provide the common defense, promote general Welfare, and secure the Blessings of Liberty to ourselves and our Prosperity, do ordain and establish this Constitution for the United States of America."

This document does not define government powers or individual rights, it merely states the principles on which we stand on as a people… United.

The most memorable and impactful times of my life were during my service in the United States Army. I was fortunate to see America for what it can be. I saw Americans standing in solidarity. I saw Americans supporting each other and their families. I saw Americans from across the nation with different backgrounds and cultures brokering lifelong friendships. I saw Americans caring for one another. But most of all, I saw Americans defending freedom with many of them paying the ultimate sacrifice in the process. I saw America.

I will share with you a story about how racism was destroyed by unity and an unwavering will of a unit that was bonded by the American Spirit. A young private arrived at his first active-duty unit with high expectations and supreme confidence. The Soldier was filled with pride and a gigantic sense of accomplishment having graduated from basic training and advanced individual training.

A few months after arriving, the unit was notified that it would be deploying to the Middle East in support of Operation Desert Shield. There was only about ten months until the unit would depart so as you can imagine, the unit began to train to prepare for the deployment. So here goes, the Soldier was a driver for the Unit First Sergeant in a Field Artillery Unit.

Typically, Field Artillery units will maneuver mainly at night (from dusk to dawn). After a long night of training, the Soldier drove the unit First Sergeant back to the unit's field headquarters arriving around 6AM. The Soldier was given orders by the First Sergeant to refuel the vehicle, get some breakfast, and lastly camo and park the vehicle before heading to his hooch (tent or field quarters) to sleep. It is standard by the way that all drivers get a required amount of sleep between shifts or movements (varies with situation).

The Soldier followed the orders given. While headed to the field tent or quarters, the Soldier was stopped by the Company Executive Officer (a 2nd Lieutenant). The lieutenant said, "I need you to get the vehicle ready and meet me in 10 mikes, we are headed out for field maneuvers". The Soldier was confused, but knew that no matter what, you follow the last order given by superiors.

The Soldier was spotted by the Unit First Sergeant while preparing the vehicle and angrily shouted, "what the hell are you doing Soldier? I thought I told you to eat some chow and bed down?" The Soldier, sensing being in an impossible situation, decided to attempt to explain to the First Sergeant what was happening and why. The First Sergeant abruptly closed the conversation out and told the Soldier to park that vehicle and go back to bed until 1600 unless he says otherwise. The Soldier followed the order and returned to the sleep tent.

The Soldier was soundly asleep for about 20 minutes when the lieutenant arrived and awakened the Soldier shouting, "Get the hell up! I told you to be ready an hour ago!" The Soldier, naturally terrified of getting in trouble, especially with an officer, tried to explain what happened and why. The lieutenant, in a rage, flipped the cot over with the Soldier in it, sending the Soldier to the ground. The lieutenant crouched over the Soldier and shouted, "Listen nigger, you do what I tell you to do, don't give me any fucking lip".

The Soldier, in what was described as uncontrollable rage, attacked the young officer with a flurry of punches. The scuffle was quickly broken up by others that had witnessed this altercation. The Soldier was restrained and removed from the tent. The military police arrived on the scene and arrested the Soldier. Before departing the training area, the First Sergeant stopped the military police to learn the details of the matter. The military police stated that the lieutenant wanted to press charges for assault in hopes of the Soldier being convicted in a court martial. He was quoted by one of the witnesses as saying, "I want that nigger to fry in the electric chair".

The First Sergeant urged the military police to release the Soldier to him and that he would resolve this matter at the unit level. The military police got authorization to release the Soldier to the command shortly thereafter. The Commanding Officer and the First Sergeant began to gather details that led up to the event. The First Sergeant was a key figure in the resolution of all of this. He immediately came to the defense of the Soldier stating that "the Soldier was following orders". However, the Soldier was still not in the clear. The assault charge was still a very real possibility.

After reviewing the statements of witnesses, the Commander and the First Sergeant concluded with appropriate action. The Military Police, the Soldier, and the Lieutenant were summoned to headquarters that evening. In an unexpected twist, the Soldier was given the opportunity to file assault charges against the officer for flipping the cot over with the Soldier in it. The Soldier was also given the opportunity to file Equal Opportunity complaints against the lieutenant for his disparaging and racist remarks.

This ordeal on the surface would normally have an unfortunate outcome for one or both parties involved. There is nothing wrong with democracy or the spirit of America; with work..., it works. The outcome was vindication for the Soldier as the young officer took a plea -

either face court martial (same as the Soldier) for assault or drop the charges and resign his commission in lieu of separation from the military. Obviously, he took the latter.

The takeaway from this is the conditions were all present for this situation to go haywire. It took place on a military base in the Southeast in 1989. The Soldier was a 19-year-old African American who grew up in the 70s in the deep south. The lieutenant was a 22-year-old college graduate from rural Louisiana, from a generational wealthy family with strong ties to white supremacists. It is astounding that the lieutenant had the mindset to abuse his authority and rank to discriminate against the Soldier blatantly and racially in 1989 at 22 years old. This was a perfect example of learned behavior. It is ironic though, logically speaking, I would imply that America can learn how to be intolerable to all that BS in the same manner.

The US military includes males, females, transgender individuals, and people of all origins and races. There is a unique culture for each of those individuals to thrive and serve with honor. Since I was in the Army (Beat Navy, by the way), my description of this culture is One Color (Green), One Gender (Soldier).

There is more, but first let me let you in on another little secret. All military personnel (active, reserve, retired, and veterans) absolutely love to talk about the wonder years of their time serving. A good bit of it is some of the most unbelievable things you will ever hear. Add a couple of cold ones and you will begin to experience some of the greatest tales ever told (LIES). I will only share non-alcoholic experiences and stay away from the fictional versions.

The Army, like other branches of service, has seven core values. They are the foundation and core of the culture:

- Loyalty

- Duty

- Respect

- Selfless Service

- Honor

- Integrity

- Personal Courage

Each of these values has their distinct individual definitions. When combined, the description or depiction is an American Soldier. From day one, these values become your guiding light. I will share with you how those values changed the hearts and minds of some Soldiers that I encountered during my career.

My last assignment prior to retiring from the military was at Fort Johnson (formerly known as Fort Polk), Louisiana. It was the most challenging position I had ever faced. There were over two hundred Soldiers under my charge as the unit First Sergeant. The first thing I noticed when I arrived was how severely fractured the culture was. I heard stories about the duty assignment my whole career. It was one of those places that was not atop the list of places you wanted to be.

I was working late one evening when I got a call from the Staff Duty Sergeant (leader in charge of the living quarters of Soldiers for the evening). He informed me that the military police were on the scene and that one of our Soldiers was a victim of attempted vehicular homicide. The Soldier was married and allegedly she was visiting another Soldier at the barracks whom she, once again allegedly, had been secretly dating. I rushed to the barracks to assess what happened and to ensure everyone was safe.

Upon my arrival, I was met by a Soldier that was serving as the runner for the Staff Duty Sergeant (typically duties include being an assistant to the Staff Duty Sergeant for the evening). I asked, "Where is the staff duty?" The Soldier replied, "doing a statement with the police First Sergeant". I then asked, "Can you tell me what happened?"

What happened next had me at a loss for words, and I did not really have time to deal with it right away until I knew the status of my injured Soldier. She was okay but she did suffer some severe injuries to her legs. So back to the matter, the Soldier's response to what he had witnessed completely threw me off. He says, "I saw the whole thing. I was out here smoking when the car came speeding through the parking lot. A colored fella was driving and mowed down that colored girl when she and another fella were coming out of the barracks".

Just so you completely understand, the Soldier I was talking to was eighteen years old, and the year was 2009. I was flabbergasted when he said that. I had to ask, "Did you say the Soldier was colored?" He looked me square in the eye and said, "Yes First Sergeant". I asked, "Are you sure?" He replied again, "Yes First Sergeant, I saw the whole thing". So finally, I asked, "Well, what color am I?" The look on his face was as innocent as a toddler. It was that exact moment that I realized; this kid really does not realize what he is saying is wrong.

I dismissed the Soldier so that he could return to his post and went to speak with the Staff Duty Sergeant and the military police. The next duty day I summoned the Soldier and his supervisor to my office. I proceeded to talk to him about the incident and praised him for being alert and responsive. His detailed account of the events was key in apprehending the offender. My main motive was to dig deeper into the Soldier's background.

I found out that the Soldier was from a very small town in southern Mississippi. He had never been around African Americans until he joined the military. The term colored when describing African Americans apparently was the norm in and around his community. I could not believe that this kid would know what that was. It was learned behavior.

I asked the Soldier, "Are you a racist?" He replied, "No First Sergeant. I joined the Army to get away from all of that." I believed him. I could tell that it was not in his heart, but he had been exposed to a repulsive culture his whole life. This was the perfect training opportunity. I instructed his supervisor to immediately begin ethics training with this Soldier. There remained one unanswered question, why is it that this

Soldier that has now been around African American Soldiers for at least a year now comfortably using that language?

The answer... there were leaders within my organization that allowed this foolishness to happen. The happy ending of all this was made possible by those seven Army Values. Education and desegregation are weapons of mass success. That Soldier went on to become one of the brightest and most respected Soldiers in the unit. But there was still an enormous amount of work to be done. My focus shifted to subordinate leadership. I needed to rid my unit of this cancer as quickly as possible.

The demographics of the unit were odd, to say the least. There was not a lot of diversity within the senior leadership. I began to prioritize getting to know my subordinate leaders. Boy, did I have my work cut out for me! I knew I had this cultural nightmare to deal with, but more importantly, we were gearing up for a yearlong deployment to Afghanistan in support of Operation Enduring Freedom. Time was of the essence. I knew that I needed my unit to be an airtight cohesive team going into this deployment.

I heeded the advice given to me by one of my mentors when I was coming up through the ranks. I applied the three attributes of a leader:

BE – being true to oneself, honest, and resolute.

KNOW – know yourself and seek self-improvement.

DO – stand for what is right by being actionable, Deeds not Words.

The one thing that gave me confidence was that no matter the rank or what level of responsibility you achieve; Soldiers will follow good leaders to the moon. My first target was one of my more seasoned leaders. This Staff Sergeant had served around 14 years or so with numerous deployments under his belt. His performance records were decent; however, the one thing I quickly noticed was a weakness in communication. I invited this Staff Sergeant to play golf with me a few times to assess his character. It was very productive. The thing that we immediately found we had in common was that we suck at golf (him more than me though, I kicked his ass).

I shared with him the details of the incident involving the Soldier being injured at the barracks. There had been rumblings around the unit that he was one of the leaders that fostered this culture. He was never directly promoting it but was not taking the initiative to stop it either.

This was another training opportunity for me. He revealed to me that it was the culture when he arrived and that although he did not feel comfortable with it, he felt as if he would be targeted by senior leaders who supported this behavior if he spoke out about it. I understood where he came from, but I also reminded him of his obligation as a leader. Those Army Values like Personal Courage, Integrity, Duty, and Honor should have been ringing as loud as the Liberty Bell inside his head. I told him that we simply cannot allow isolated ignorance to become systemic. He did not realize that his immobility and silence were pouring fuel on the fire.

Lessons learned from our engagement became infectious and spread throughout the unit like wildfire. The new narrative was, in my unit it did not matter if you are African American, White American, Latin American, Asia American, Native American, or even Red Neck American, we are all One Color (Green), One Gender (Soldier).

The once morally compromised unit was now the example of what a winning team looks like.

Unfortunately, every champion will be tested. We certainly were not immune to this. In the road ahead we would face some enormous challenges. The mental toll and veracity of deployment is a hard hill to climb. It is not all doom and gloom though. The bond you develop with those who were once strangers becomes eternal.

Remember the young Soldier that once referred to African Americans as colored? He married an African American Soldier and has kids now. I bet you did not see that coming! So here is how this thing became full circle. What I am about to tell you is very personal. This has and will continue to stick with me for the rest of my life.

In August of 2011 (on my birthday), I was at the company headquarters when I heard over the radio that a medivac was incoming. First, let me say, it is always a somber feeling anytime you hear that. The call revealed that a particular convoy had been attacked and that there were severe injuries. The convoy identified was that of my Soldiers. I rushed over to the field hospital to meet the incoming helicopter. It was confirmed that three of my Soldiers had been severely injured and would require immediate surgery. The absolute hardest thing I ever had to do was to watch through a window as those medical personnel worked to save those Soldiers' lives. I felt helplessness, hopelessness, sorrow, and anger all at the same time. It was a terrible feeling watching the emotions of those fellow Soldiers being trampled by the conditions of war. It is one of the most personable feelings I have ever had.

Amid the most tragic event to date, I was called back to headquarters urgently. There was another mission that had to be completed right away. I still cannot believe how I was able to gather myself to transition to that task. My only concern at that time was those three warriors lying in those hospital beds fighting for their lives. I was given a directive to send another mission out. I could not believe what I was being asked to do. I mean, this was the worst day ever, the hardest decision I have made in my lifetime.

With my heart pounding a million beats a minute, I mustered the team and gave that order. The most improbable thing happened during the convoy briefing. I thought that those Soldiers would be terrified and not be mentally fit to roll out. The undeniable, unwavering, and determined spirit of these young Soldiers emerged with laser-sharp focus. The word unity is undervalued. These Soldiers, some of which were once racially, gender, and socially divided were one.

The power of unity has been on display in our country for centuries. The message of unity is everlasting. I challenge you to be about "we." Of course, we are all different, but it should not take an event for us to stand in unison. In the words of Parliament-Funkadelic, we are… "One Nation Under a Groove, Getting down for the Funk of it". The voices and actions of many in unison create the most unconventional, complex, yet simplistic math formula, (the only time where 1 plus more than one equals 1).

CHAPTER 3

TRANSITION & UNPACKING THE IMPACT OF WAR

Separation and/or retirement from the military is undoubtedly a pivotal time in a veteran's life. The uncertainty of the next chapter can be overwhelming. Everything changes in an instant. The revelation of knowing that, although I served the nation with honor, it is also how I supported my family.

It is only natural that parts of the life you once lived transition over with you to civilian life. Personally speaking, this was and continues to be at times, an enormous challenge. I assumed that the structure and culture of the military would be the norm and that civilians would welcome me with open arms. Reality set in quickly. It felt like it was a Walker kick (Walker Texas Ranger).

I found myself suddenly living in a world that just does not value anything. Everyone seemed to be so entitled and unwilling. Work seemed optional, and accountability was non-existent. But here comes the Walker Kick combo; it was astonishing to see just how Un-Patriotic and Un-United the country really was. I recall attending an NBA basketball game shortly after I retired, and the National Anthem was being played. With no hesitation at all, I went to the position of attention with my hand over my heart. As the song was playing, I began to see people still sitting, walking around, conversating, chugging beers, and carrying on as if they did not care about what was taking place. I was thinking to myself "if this game was on a military installation, I would be chewing some ass right now!" What the hell are these people doing, I thought. I honestly could not process what I was witnessing.

My thoughts were, if this is what life is going to be like going forward, it is going to be very difficult. What would be my strategy? First let me say that by no means am I qualified to give any professional or clinical directives to anyone. I did, however, realize that I could not do it alone. The world was not going to conform to the culture of the military. Those twenty plus years were merely (although very important) a chapter in my life. For me to survive, I would need to adapt to this new culture. If you have not sought out any professional assistance, I encourage it. It is nothing to be ashamed of. It helps me process my thoughts in a way that fuels growth. The road is long, but I think about some wise words once spoken by the late Kobe Bryant...

"It is not about the destination; it is about the journey."

Those words resonate with me. No one really knows what the future holds. The only thing we can control is what we do today to prepare for tomorrow. As I began this journey, it seemed as if I was not going to make it. Those feelings of depression and isolation forever changed my quality of life.

Do you remember what I said about unity? It came through for me like Jordan in a game seven. My wife......, there are no words to describe how much she means to me. I often tell her that she saved my life. She always has this puzzled look on her face when I say it. To have someone in your corner, not really knowing all the details of what happened to you, cannot be underappreciated. Like a battle buddy, she knows my strengths and weaknesses. She is about we, and without her, there is no us. I absolutely love her.

Family and friends are essential to combatting the anxiety that comes with leaving the military. They can help you begin to recognize the person in the mirror. My grandkids know that I served, but they see me as Papa. Let me explain how essential that recognition is to me. If they see me as a regular person, logically I assume this is how I am viewed by others. Simple enough, right?

Nope! It is only one piece of the whole transition process. There must be a balance between my military bearing and my true character. I am proud of my military service, but it was huge for me to realize and not lose sight that it was voluntary. I do not expect anyone to shower me with praise every time they see me. Naturally, anyone would be pleased to hear such, but I realized that was who I was then, and this is who I am now. I am at a different stage of the journey. The quality of my life does not depend on acceptance.

To be honest, and it is different for every veteran, I am sure, but I am embracing Tim every day. I have no desire to deal with being First Sergeant Harvey or Drill Sergeant Harvey. Many of my former colleagues have yet to embrace who they are. The transition never got off the ground. Many live near and around military bases, with military or government jobs. There is absolutely nothing wrong with that if you can understand that you are no longer serving and that you are now employed. There is a stark difference!

Separation anxiety is a real thing. Some of these people simply cannot adjust, and that is okay too. Here lies the problem though, without recognition that you choose to stay in your comfort zone, culturally you hinder your ability to adapt to the real world. The reason for this is that you will not expose yourself to anything outside the military culture.

I know veterans who have separated from the military but still use a military signature block in their emails, even though they now have Hotmail email addresses instead of military ones. See what I am saying? Who still uses Hotmail? Remember that ball game I was talking about? Why did I see a veteran with that jersey tucked into those jeans? Is it necessary to have your military rank and jump wings on your vehicle bumper when you already have disabled veteran tags that should suffice?

This behavior is not at all strange to those who served because we realize that you are still serving in your own way. I am only joking; in my experience, every veteran celebrates other veterans. Not everyone can serve in the military, and they have my respect regardless of how peculiar those outfits may be at times.

Seriously, I wish I could say the same for everyone. There are Americans who do not appreciate the service of African American veterans at all. That impressive part of your life's resume holds no water in real-world situations.

Not because it is totally insignificant; it's just that civilians have not been a part of anything like that before. When I served, many highlights of my career were displayed on my dress uniform. A trained eye could quickly determine what type of soldier I was. Being an African American veteran, I have been a victim of how America, at times, perceives me more times than I can count.

My wife and I were out early one morning running errands and decided to stop by a local coffee shop. I parked in front of the establishment as she went in to get us coffee. Like most combat veterans, I parked by backing up into the space. The space was designated for handicapped/disabled parking. I did not violate any laws by parking there because my wife and I are disabled veterans, and our vehicle's license plates bear those designations as well. I noticed two white men in a car looking in my direction. One was on the phone, and the other was slowly driving by and pointing in my direction. The car circled the building and entered the drive-through lane. After about two minutes, two police officers arrived on the scene. They boxed my vehicle and got out with their weapons drawn, one on each side of my vehicle. The officer on my left side yelled, "Get out of the car, sir!" I calmly asked why I was being asked to exit the vehicle, but he ignored me and repeated his command.

By now, I was thinking this could escalate quickly. I tried to speak calmly to the officer to calm him down as I began to exit the vehicle, not wanting to provoke him with his weapon drawn. Before I could open the door to exit, I saw the other officer coming around to the driver's side and giving a throat slash signal to the first officer, as if to signal that everything was clear. I assume that he had noticed my license plate identifying me as a disabled veteran. The original officer then asked for some identification. I provided both my driver's license and military identification. My wife, returning to the vehicle after seeing the commotion, witnessed all that was happening. The officers reviewed my identification and without any explanation or hesitation, holstered their weapons, returned my identification, and simply said, "have a nice day" with a smirk. As they departed, I saw the two men who had been watching, seemingly entertained by the situation. My wife and I were infuriated and mortified by what had just taken place.

Now let us break this down to gain a full understanding. Here is the situation: I, a Black man, was driving a nice vehicle and parked legally in a designated handicapped/disabled spot. Two white men noticed me there, observing me quietly. I had a hunch they might have called the police due to their peculiar and unsettling behavior. While I can't confirm this, the reality across the nation is that innocent African Americans have faced assault and even death at the hands of the police in similar scenarios.

Those two men had no knowledge of my background, and it seemed they didn't care. They didn't consider that their actions could potentially lead to a tragic outcome involving law enforcement. Or perhaps, deep down, did they feel entitled to call the police on any Black person they suspected of breaking "their law"? It all sounds sadly familiar, doesn't it?

I can hear my grandmother's voice in my head saying, "If you're gonna tell it, tell it all." Let's not overlook those sworn to protect us. Those officers behaved disgracefully, reveling in my humiliation. Their brazen abuse of power echoed the darkest days of the Jim Crow South. Despite my status as a decorated retired disabled veteran with nearly twenty-five years of service and three combat tours under my belt, they treated me as if I were a field hand in 1860 at that moment. The fact that I am a veteran should have been irrelevant, yet even after confirming my legitimacy, their attitude remained unchanged. I couldn't help but wonder, "Would they have treated a white veteran in the same disrespectful manner?"

I managed to get through that harrowing incident with a wounded spirit, another chapter in my journey of transitioning into civilian life. I knew this wouldn't be the only challenge, but the frequency of such challenges caught me off guard.

Another encounter unfolded when my wife and I were parking at a grocery store in a handicapped/disabled spot. As I stepped out and went around to assist my wife, an elderly white couple approached. The man stopped behind my vehicle, inspecting my license plate, and then turned to me, saying, "This spot is for handicapped folks." I replied, "I am aware, sir, it's for handicapped and/or disabled people. Do you have trouble understanding what the license plate indicates?" His response was dismissive, "No, I get it just fine, but you sure don't look disabled to me." My wife, sensing the brewing tension and ignorance from the man in his 45 hat and matching t-shirt, wordlessly urged me to leave. Feeling the weight of his bigotry, I retorted, "You don't look foolish, yet here we are."

I was determined not to let that man affect me the same way the police incident did. I am grateful for my wife, who serves as my safety net in these situations. Despite feeling a strong urge to physically retaliate in both instances, I am aware of the dire consequences, knowing that everything is on the line for me and my family.

Throughout my transition to civilian life, I've learned to identify triggers that can sway my day towards goodness or ruin. Veterans often struggle with unpacking the impact of war, and as an African American Veteran, the compounding social inequalities only add to the weight I carry.

There are moments when life feels overwhelmingly heavy. Memories of deployments linger, with certain thoughts, sounds, and even smells from those times haunting me to this day. Driving under overpasses or bridges triggers anxiety due to their past use as strategic spots for targeting American forces, with the enemy dropping grenades onto approaching convoys.

Fireworks, once joy-filled symbols of celebration, now evoke memories of constant mortar attacks. The sharp crack of gunpowder in the air brings back echoes of past encounters with the enemy. Even the smell of diesel fuel or gasoline can momentarily transport me back to specific moments or incidents.

As I mentioned earlier, the tragic events of August 24, 2010, which coincidentally is my birthday, marked a significant shift in my life. Previously, I celebrated my birthday surrounded by loved ones like anyone else. Since that day, August 24th has transformed into a time of reflection, sadness, and gratitude. In the military, leaders often express their care for their soldiers; in my case, my sentiments towards them mirror that of a father for his children - they are all family to me.

Outside of therapy, I haven't shared much about myself and my well-being. I believe it's crucial for veterans to understand that the challenges we face are not exclusive. Here's a part of my journey that I hope can shed some light:

There are mornings when I wake up and look in the mirror, and the person staring back seems unfamiliar. To clarify, it's not a dementia-related issue but rather a deeper introspection. In combat, I was exposed to incredibly dangerous situations. Images of burned and mutilated bodies of civilians, including women and children who were non-combatants, haunt me. I have witnessed decapitations, torture, starvation, and displacement - experiences that slowly erode one's soul. The human mind is not meant to endure and process such atrocities. Rarely does a day pass without reminders of the places I served. Some days intrusive thoughts or emotional turmoil make sleep terrifying, as dreams blend reality, leaving me afraid to sleep.

My wife has recounted witnessing disturbing behaviors during my sleep that I have no recollection of upon waking.

Every day feels like a journey of self-discovery as I navigate changes in my appearance, desires, diet, hobbies, relationships, and even my own thoughts and perceptions. It's a constant battle to safeguard my mental health, a battle I must win, no matter how taxing it may be.

The lingering impacts of war are formidable and undefeated. Openly acknowledging how these experiences affect me has been crucial for my survival. During my visits to my mental health professional, the question "Have you thought about or tried to commit suicide in the last thirty days?" has become a regular inquiry. For years, my immediate response was "no." However, after subsequent deployments, that answer shifted. While I've never felt compelled to take my own life, I had been deceiving myself by denying thoughts of suicide. My recent response has been, "Yes, I have considered it. I do not have plans or urges to act on it, but each day presents a unique challenge." Knowing that my family, friends, and comrades rely on me empowers me to keep fighting.

Despite facing physical and verbal assaults, discrimination, or racial profiling, I hold onto the determination to persevere. For this reason, I keep my internal compass - my GPS - set on forward motion, ensuring that I keep moving forward.

CHAPTER 4

NAVIGATING CONVERSATIONS

It is every parent's inherent responsibility to set conditions for their children and grandchildren to live the American Dream. Unfortunately, the obstacles in doing so are different for African American families. Systemic problems will not end with reactions to individual circumstances. The system must change.

Often, we are directed to deviate from our usual route during our travels. When the GPS says, "Recalculating Route", the reactions can vary. You could be overwhelmingly happy at the fact you may save time and elude heavy traffic, or you could get angry at the fact you have to travel a less desirable route to continue your journey. You may discover that the GPS lost the signal, and you were temporarily disconnected.

Despite the circumstances, the main objective is to have a plan to get moving. The laws of the land serve as the GPS that will generally guide us in the right direction. As we encounter obstacles or find ourselves in a place where we are diverted (recalculating route), we can stop if needed, and analyze the best course of action before proceeding.

Let us go back to and reference my encounter with the police at the coffee shop. Here is an example of how an incident like that differs among races in America.

Scenario Number 1:

A young white male/female parked legally in a handicapped slot waiting for their companion to return with coffee. The police would arrive on the scene and conduct a routine traffic violation stop given any unforeseen circumstances. They would not feel the need to approach the scene with weapons drawn. They would have verified credentials and been on their way. For this reason, white parents are not too concerned about their children having an encounter with the police. The worst that could happen here was the young male/female receiving a ticket.

Scenario Number 2:

An African American young male/female parked legally in a handicapped spot waiting for their companion to return with coffee. The police arrived on the scene with weapons drawn. The young male/female knows immediately that this is a life-or-death situation. Any little thing can be perceived as threatening and could provoke the officers. This is an African American parent's worst nightmare. What advice can you give other than to stay calm in a situation like that? I can tell you from personal experience, it is impossible to be calm. At that moment, being black hits you like a ton of bricks.

I know that this situation seems dire, but it is the harsh reality of how things are. The advice to stay calm is all that we can offer to our youth and others that may find themselves in a situation like that. I offer this one advantage; realize that if you are African American, it is not a matter of if you will ever be racially profiled or discriminated against, it is when. In knowing this, you can prepare yourself mentally and have a plan to navigate through that situation successfully. The plan must be one that ends in a peaceful and non-fatal solution. Survival is the most crucial element of the situation. Any legal ramifications that may or may not occur need to be secondary.

I spoke earlier about democracy being evolutionary. Change can derail (or recalculate) ugly scenarios such as these. Sometimes the culture allows for dreadful things to happen. The recalculated route often yields unforeseen circumstances. The opportunity for predators of the free society to ambush those traveling recalculated routes is always possible and should never be forgotten. Heed every warning and follow your instincts in uncertain areas. Every day we have an opportunity to make tomorrow better.

Do you remember the situation I spoke of earlier with the young nineteen-year-old white Soldier referencing African Americans as colored? That was a fitting example of learned behavior. He was not born that way. Children have what I call racial innocence. They are ignorant of the ugliness of discrimination. The Army introduced that young Soldier to equality and what democracy represents.

I am thankful that I had the opportunity to retrain and reshape a flaw in this young man's character. I realized that his GPS had been rerouted early on.

I challenge every American to envision where they, along with their children and loved ones, want to go. Think about what it will take to get there. Set your course and get moving. You will be pleasantly surprised to see how many people across all races and cultures traveling the same path seeking the same goals and opportunities. This is what really makes America great (no pun intended)!

The military afforded me the opportunity to become domestically and internationally culturally diverse. My biggest takeaway was, whether it was in large cities, small towns or villages, mountains, or even more remote places, people still had basic common needs and desires. They all wanted the chance to provide for themselves and their families. They wanted their children to be safe and healthy. They wanted the freedom to navigate their individual journeys.

Our responsibility to the younger generations of Americans is to teach them to denounce anything and everything that divides us. It sounds a bit cliché, but we are all in this together. The dream that Dr. Martin Luther King Jr. had of young black children and young white children joining hands as brothers and sisters became a reality. It is time for all of us to wake up from the American Dream and reshape the American Reality. Our future and the future of our children depend on it.

The Transportation Corps of the United States Army has a catchy slogan that reads, *"Nothing Happens Until Something Moves."*

Words like democracy, equality, unity, and prosperity have no meaning without the actions of those who speak about them.

CHAPTER 5

THE AMERICAN REALITY AND THE POWER OF ACCOUNTABILITY

It cannot be overstated that in life evolution is inevitable. Life is evolutionary. Change can be good, bad, or indifferent, but it will occur. During my life, I have become accustomed to effecting change when the opportunity is there to do so.

The social, racial, and economic obstacles that divide our nation are part of the cycle of life that can be altered. America has withstood some dark days. Who knows what lies ahead? The good news is that change is actionable. It is a verb. America can make the dreams of the late Reverend Doctor Martin Luther King Jr. a reality. For that to happen, though, the spawn of slavery must be eradicated. Those who wish to impose a life of servitude on fellow Americans must be held accountable for their actions. It all starts with the truth. To create and sustain that more perfect union referenced in the Preamble of the Constitution of the United States, America must walk the talk.

In my lifetime, I have witnessed things that are wrong in every way possible, yet and still it happens. America cannot lose its moral compass. Accountability is not just the admission of wrongdoing; it is also initiative and responsibility. Ponder this: the Confederacy was a treasonous act and flat-out domestic terrorism. This is not hyperbole. I cannot understand why this is even a debate. Why would we allow those individuals and those states that seceded to return to the union without any consequences? Then we allowed them (during reconstruction) to adopt laws that would allow the segregation and discrimination of African American citizens for over a half-century. It was not until the Voting Rights Act of 1965 was passed that African Americans could vote without being racially discriminated against, or so we thought.

The late Congressman and iconic Civil Rights Activist, John R. Lewis, proposed (named after him) the Voting Rights Advancement Act of 2023. This bill was designed to strengthen and restore parts of the original Voting Rights Act of 1965. Yep, I know what you are thinking and have the same question! What changed in the original bill, why did it change, and what legislative chain of custody supports that change?

It will come as no surprise when I tell you that there are some who wish to roll back the hands of time to the good old days of the Jim Crow South. Now that we have identified the problem, let me offer a solution.

STOP IT, AMERICA!

Stop allowing those who oppose the laws of the land that support freedom and inclusion for all citizens to violate the rights of others with unlawful discriminatory practices. Stop allowing elected officials to hide behind immoral rules of politics. Stop allowing the religious beliefs of white evangelicals to become laws that target other American citizens for their beliefs. Stop allowing the public display of anything (statues, flags, memorials) that depicts or represents the Confederacy.

For those who argue it's about heritage, consider this: Those people were not American heroes. Your right to display that was given to you by those who served and protected this nation. Spoiler alert: many of those individuals are African Americans who do not appreciate being reminded of a time when their ancestors were enslaved. That heritage that makes you proud represents one of humanity's greatest sins.

Next up is the Second Amendment, a key political talking point in our nation. This constitutional right has been exploited and re-engineered to appeal to those who wish to divide our country. Politicians twist its meaning to sow discord, camouflaging their true motives for needing access to so many weapons.

Indulge me here, as I grew up in the seventies in the Deep South. It was common to see white men riding around in pickup trucks with rifles on gun racks. This evolved to men showing up in supermarkets with pistols displayed openly. While all legal, it's worth noting the South has always seemed to operate under different rules.

If an African American man possessed a weapon in public in 1975, he would undoubtedly face police apprehension or even violence. The right to bear arms wouldn't have mattered; he would be perceived as a threat. Unfortunately, not much has changed today.

I personally have a concealed carry permit for my firearm, obtained legally after passing a background check. In a supermarket one morning, I encountered a armed white man, passing by me and two other individuals. Subsequently, I noticed an elderly white lady's terrified reaction upon seeing my firearm, causing concern.

As I envisioned potential consequences, fearing police confrontation, thankfully, it did not escalate. Reflecting on this experience, I noted the inconsistency in reactions between the white man openly carrying a firearm and myself. Despite no threatening behavior, the discrepancy in responses based on race was stark.

Having laid out these details of the ordeal, it's evident that despite similar actions, different reactions occurred based on race. Addressing this problem, a solution will now be offered.

"Stop it, America!

For African Americans, something as simple as being racially profiled and perceived as a threat because of the color of your skin can lead to innocent, law-abiding Americans being killed by police. Too much? That is exactly the point. I certainly cannot afford to take things like this lightly. This is an unfortunate reality that we need to address.

Time for some truth about the Second Amendment. At no time, past or present, was it meant for civilians to own weapons such as high-powered semi-automatic and fully automatic Assault Rifles and handguns. It was ratified on December 15, 1791, as a law that protects the right to keep and bear arms. I will say that again, the year was 1791! We are talking about a time when single-shot muskets were the hot ticket. It was not until 2008 that the Supreme Court of the United States (District of Columbia v. Heller) affirmed for the first time that the right belongs to individuals for self-defense in the home. The ruling also states that the right is not unlimited and, I quote, 'Does not preclude the existence of certain long-standing prohibitions, such as those forbidding the possessions of firearms by felons and the mentally ill or restrictions on the carrying of dangerous and unusual weapons.'

The American people have endured so many horrific mass shootings to the point it has become the norm. Lives are being lost, yet we have not done anything to stop this senseless violence. This is America. Our nation leads the world in gun violence, disgraceful. The people that we elect to serve as part of our governing body have the power to stop this. Those that choose to manipulate the Second Amendment for political gain are funded by corporations that make billions from gun sales each year. Money, power, and the quest for racial superiority have eaten away at the moral fibers of the Second Amendment. I can tell you firsthand from serving in the military that many of the weapons used are for one thing, mass casualties. There are no logical explanations for a civilian to have the ability to legally purchase any assault-style or mass casualty type of weapon. I am sick to my stomach every time there is a school shooting at the hands of someone armed with one of these weapons. Again, I ask, what changed in the original bill, why did it change, and what legislative chain of custody supports that change?"

The preservation of the Union is the responsibility of every American. Democracy has an auto-correct function in its DNA that is self-charging, auto-replenishing, and with a little maintenance, high-performance capable of yielding amazing results. That function is the right to vote. Voting is the most impactful way to affect change. Voting has an impeccable record in our history. The Constitution of the United States of America was created on the foundation of voting. Perhaps the greatest changes via voting in the history of America were those that happened during the Civil Rights Movement.

Democracy cannot survive without voting. It is the ultimate check and balance to adhering to the will of the people. Now that we have identified the problem, I will offer a solution. VOTE, AMERICA! The most consistently actionable thing one can do to affect change is voting. I may not be able to change the world, but I have no room to complain about anything if I do not let my voice be heard. Who knows, my thoughts may be those of others that wish to affect change. The future is shaped by the events of the past. If we do not learn from America's history, we are bound to repeat it.

With this poem, I bid you adieu...

"Un-United"

From the ashes of a dream, a nightmare was unfolding,

A lifetime of hardship and suffering, for a race that was imploding,

A nation of freedom and prosperity was the vision for the land,

But inclusion in that vision was not for every man,

Generations of servitude for those that were oppressed,

With no one to turn to in their time of distress,

Humanity turned its back on one of its own,

A racial identity in an instant, turned to stone,

Second Class citizenship, was my ancestral point of origin,

The nation was built on the backs of those who are still considered foreign,

Evolution is inevitable, and often undeniable,

Contrary and deliberate, to those that view it as undesirable,

As the world watched, before our very eyes,

Equality came like the sun, clearing cloudy skies,

The war seems eternal, yet we continue to fight it,

Or the country will remain as it began, Un-United.

Timothy Harvey
Love, Peace, & Soul

Epilogue:

As the sun sets on the final pages of "Un-United," Timothy Harvey's voice lingers, a poignant echo urging us to forge a new path forward. Through the poignant lens of his lived experiences and the wisdom gained from a lifetime dedicated to service, Timothy leaves us with a crucial question echoing in our hearts: How can we redefine unity in a fractured world?

In his final words, Timothy Harvey doesn't offer easy answers or quick fixes. Instead, he leaves us with a challenge, a call to action resonating with the urgency of our times. He reminds us that unity isn't just a lofty ideal but a tangible reality within our grasp if only we have the courage to confront our biases, acknowledge our shared history, and embrace the transformative power of empathy and understanding.

As we turn the last page of "Un-United," we are not merely closing a book but opening a new chapter in the ongoing narrative of building a more inclusive, just, and united society. Timothy's journey may be over, but the legacy of his words will continue to inspire generations to come.

Dedication:

This book is dedicated to the people who have served or are currently serving in our nation's armed forces. I am hopeful that this book will inspire you to embrace the next chapter of your life. I would also like to recognize the families of those service members and veterans, who play a vital role in the reintegration of service members/veterans into the world.

First and foremost, I want to extend my heartfelt gratitude to my beautiful wife, Simone, for her undying love and unwavering support. As I have expressed many times before, you saved my life. I love you endlessly.

I offer my deepest thanks to my mother, Verla Harvey, a resilient single mom who overcame immense challenges to raise and provide for her children. Mom, your strength and love have guided me through life. I love you dearly.

To Brittany, Maiya, and Wynter, you are the light of my life. Your presence fills my days with joy and purpose. I love you all to the moon and back.

Lastly, this book is dedicated to the memory of my mother-in-law, the late Peggyann Godfrey, and our aunt, the late Emily Smith. Your spirits continue to reside in our hearts, forever cherished and remembered.

Printed in the USA
CPSIA information can be obtained
at www.ICGtesting.com
LVHW051520140524
779921LV00035B/1053/J

9 798869 293939